CW00481206

Touching Base

Dear Eileen,

Well met in Liverpool

thanks for a great

supper,

Pileen

Touching Base

Aileen La Tourette

HEADLAND

First published in 2006
by
HEADLAND PUBLICATIONS
38 York Avenue
West Kirby, Wirral
CH48 3JF

Copyright © 2006 Aileen La Tourette

British Library Cataloguing in Publication Data.
A full CIP record for this book is available from the British Library
ISBN
1 902096 95 9

*All rights reserved. No part of this publication may be
reproduced, stored in a retrieval system, or transmitted
in any form, or by any means, electronic, mechanical,
photocopying, recording or otherwise, without the prior
written permission of the publisher.*

*Requests to publish work from this book
must be sent to Headland Publications.*

*Aileen La Tourette has asserted her right under Section
77 of the Copyright, Designs and Patents Act 1988 to be
identified as the author of this book.*

Printed in Great Britain by
L. Cocker Ltd.
Unit A9, Prospect Street, Liverpool L6 1AU

HEADLAND acknowledges the financial
assistance of Arts Council England

CONTENTS

CONTENTS *continued*

Provincetown

The Pilgrim fathers almost landed here
but thought better of it, clambered
back into their sewer of a ship
rather than risk defilement
from a slipshod, zigzag coast.

They left behind one Anne Bradshaw
slipped overboard right in the harbour,
whether by accident or design,
whim, fever of love, utter fatigue
from being wife to the Governor-elect,

we'll never know. They felt their God go
silent in the drumming wind and fled
to Plymouth, more serene. William re-wed.
Anne's secret stayed in P'town.
Maybe she knew what she was doing,

maybe she felt in her bones, under her gown,
her petticoats, her corsets, filthy and rank,
she'd found her home from home,
maybe she tried to swim in, thinking to live
alone in this wild place. Maybe she did.

Touching Base

I have a bone to pick with this landscape,
- three green leaves buffed to dark gold by the sun,
beauty and poison. I stand stung,
re-crying hot tears down a mask of calamine,
give in when it's cried away, scratch.
I did it in my sleep's my alibi.

My old enemy shines like Jack Daniel's
in a glass when the light hits it. Two foes.
Booze and poison ivy. I don't do bourbon,
stick to wine, but something in this landscape
brings back the smell of smoky Jack,
like an itch I won't scratch.

Besides, I'm not here for that.
This time I'm here to catch the East Coast
from the outside, in its natural habitat.
I've tried searching houses for the past,
glass in hand, too many times.
This is a different kind of binge.

A hike. Not my style. Like I took as a kid.
I did. Literal, hairy roots climbed right out
of the ground like this across my path.
Sometimes I stumbled. I remember saddle shoes
scuffed, not meant for walking in the woods,
I was told afterwards. I remember boots, clumsy,

you couldn't run in them, and sneakers, wonderful,
the word for what I wanted to do,
sneak into the woods for the kerosene glow
from three green leaves, like it was evening
and I was inside with the flap of wings
like a match struck, with the smell of pine,

liking the way I could climb trees that were here
before me, not thinking about after I was gone,
not then. But liking my own absence certified
by their height, by their silence.
Liking my own disappearance into the woods
with its green-gold light. I like this like.

Provincetown Drugstore

It wouldn't transplant to the Champs Elysées,
or even the Big Apple. It's not Hollywood.
No one ever got discovered at the P'town
drugstore soda fountain. It's not even gay,

especially, in either sense – just a place
where regulars hang out, sipping an excuse
to be there as they watch the passing parade,
wearing their baseball caps frontwards,

folks from what's a small town, when you
get right down to it, under the gloss, dusty
as the out-of-date makeup on the shelves
behind them, dye that might turn you grey,

instead of rescue you from it. This ain't
the small-town USA that will vote Bush in
again, say no loud and clear to gay unions,
- here it seems almost quaint, not a debate.

The real issues line up at the soda fountain
with people who have nowhere else to be,
no jobs and maybe no heat in their rooms,
people whose daytime dignity depends on

the kindness of familiar strangers in libraries
and drugstores who nod, accepting them
as they plop on their stools, face the street,
the shoppers clutching bags from the boutiques.

The Marine Specialities Store, Provincetown (A Rant)

Nostalgia costs. Shingled houses, witches' hat gables,
front porches with rockers, old window sashes,
beautifully restored - the conjuring trick of small-town cosiness
owes a lot to the history and more to tourists,
wherever you find it, Provincetown or the Peloponnese.
This fishing village came from Portugal and England
to stick off the end of the USA, precariously joined,
vociferously separate. *We believe in free expression
in P'town,* says the realtor, quoting inflated prices,
seeing no contradiction. No one wants to hear it, here.
Old puritan money-myths live on under the razzamatazz,
the prosperous as the elect. Save money; money saves.
Old P'town looks away at the vulgarity: *I have, therefore I am.*
I won't admit it as I wander down Commercial Street,
but I'm looking for something long gone. I came here
from mundane New Jersey, l960ish, and it changed my life,
people painting by their garages in early light,
as we set out for a swim in the bay. People lived in
little flats with stained glass and spiral staircases that spun
stories of love without the usual constraints. I saw a way.
I also saw my mother frown and that clinched it. I was home.
P'town had shown me a bohemian rhapsody. Back now,
on sabbatical, I have the same de-conversion experience
that hit me at the Vatican, MacDougal Alley, Manhattan,
another magic place till I rediscovered it and found not grace
but money, wall-to-wall. I'm not pretending I'm immune,
in fact that's what gets me. I come in here to Marine Specialities,
dusky as a cathedral, grittier than the Unitarian billboard opposite
- which does attract, with its optimistic offerings -
Marine Specialities is more like Rome, seedy and primitive.
It's not a civilized store, with its naked approach to raw greed,
racks and barrels stuffed with cut-price lingerie, velvet gowns –

I live above the *General Store* with its eccentric range of *provisions*,
Donald in the *Package Goods* packs up my wine in brown paper bags
- you don't get friendly chin-wags in Marine Specialities.
You get old leather jackets sold by weight, fisherman's knits,
to keep out the sleet. Flannel pyjama bottoms, ten bucks,
ponchos, fifteen. Buckets of socks, a buck a pair, designer shirts,
barely singed. Going, going, gone. I never leave empty-handed,
come out blinking like I've seen a movie, *Moby Dick* maybe,
Ahab hunting the white whale at this fire sale we call a country,
spending an arm or leg, pegging up and down Commercial Street
boiling with blood-lust for something that must be here,
somewhere, antique, exquisite, cheap, must be for sale. Must be.

Seal

The town opens out after it finishes
into the Provincelands, the dunes,
paradisical beaches – but first it ends.
The bay thins, scums on top, butts float
off the side of the hotel. The jetty tries
for dignified, definite boundaries, but
there's a gritty, sewery feel out here
that says endings are never pretty.

Making for the folding waves, I think
of packing, cleaning, folding and re-
folding clothes to make more space
in the suitcase, list what remains to do
before I go. Out at the rim of town,
a seal's swum in. A big baby face lifts,
vague as a moon, for a breath, wanes.

*She had a pup yesterday, stillborn.
We took it away*, the conservationist
tells me. *We'll take her in the tank,
or her body* – the face eclipsed again
behind the cloud of shallow bay.
I can just make out a grey island
under the scum that nylons her
like a negligee as she submarines -

She came back to this rag of coast
like Demeter, for her lost pup.
Just as the word *love* pops
into my head, hers pops up,
black nose only half-clearing the slop
to blow its cluster of bubbles, gritty,
getting smaller, going, but not giving up.

Grandpère

For Thérèse

France was an idea to me, like him,
this great-grandfather who was it,
with his big nose and white hair.
France grew vegetables in the Bronx.

It was tall and thin. You took me
up strange, narrow stairs to see him.
Right away the room became an idea
I didn't like or dislike. It was curiosity

that made me look at him, lying on top
of his bed with his suit on. It made
no sense in an interesting way. Why
didn't he talk, I asked? *The talking part's*

gone up to God, you said. That made less.
We clattered down again, but he stayed.
I knew he would, by then. I knew more
than I knew, at four, or would know again.

The Blue Garden

Childhood goes on forever, mostly hidden
in rhododendron bushes, a blue garden
made of steps smoked over from a distance
by blue clouds that separate into flowers
up close, like tide going out leaving things
you can't see when it's high. Going up and
down the steps over and over, like reading
the same books, loving them again, is what
you do. Why wouldn't you? *Bush* is what
they do, and are. Flower, too, and star.
Wings sound like pages turning. Stairs are
steps and eyes looking at you, though they
tell you not to. Things aren't, aren't, fair.

Pleats

Aunt Marcelle makes the wedding gown
you try on, satin train like wearing
the staircase. *Oh no,* says Mom, *it's bad luck,*
now you might never wear it really -
but everyone gets married, don't they?

Marcelle leans over the satin, feeds it
to the machine like snow with sun gleaming
on it or real, yellowy vanilla ice cream.
A Raleigh pokes out of her red lipstick, tip
growing longer and longer, mesh of ash

ready to collapse – she dashes it away at
the last minute, laughs at your face.
Her kisses smell of smoke and sweet vermouth.
Uncle Jimmy grew up in Hell's Kitchen
where you have to give it back with interest,

but he didn't. *Sweetheart,* they call
each other. *Darling.* When they got married,
Aunt Gaby had to draw a chart.
She still tells the story when she's drunk,
how they came back twice for advice.

Uncle Jimmy always brings soft–centres
no one eats. Bridesmaids get ice-blue satin,
you, too, flower girl first in step-stop-step
down the white cloth on the long aisle,
brown hair hanging heavy down your back.

When it comes to it, your hair's cropped,
you wear pink trousers with a pleat like skirts
Marcelle used to make, a trailing cardigan
to sweep up the steps of the registry
where you don't pledge troth, but repeat

dull syllables you can't concentrate on,
find yourself thinking of Jimmy, desperately
dry-eyed, at Marcelle's funeral, white hair
cowlicky as a boy's, no shirt under his tie.
What came hard to them is the easy part.

A man will wear a pleated skirt around his neck
like a cape, in your new neighbourhood,
his dead wife's, you'll decide. Meanwhile.
back at the registry, names for pleats repeat
as you speak, words like *box* and *kick* and *knife*.

Flashbulb Memories c.1954

1.

Something lures me across the boardwalk,
my cone of shaved ice coated with root beer
or cherry syrup tight in my grip. It's a beach
we never happened on before, with people
we call, politely, Negroes – lots of them,
no one white sits on a towel, only black seats,
black backs, black arms reaching for beach-
balls, black legs running down to the water,
edging in fast or slow. I feel the icy Atlantic
fill their black belly buttons like it fills mine,
feel how crowded it is, body on body jammed
on one beach, no room for blankets spread flat,
making little camps with chairs, umbrellas,
- then Grandma touches me, says *Stop staring,*
Aileen Margaret, that's the Colored Beach.

2.

Is it a sideshow because the trailer's parked
in a side street? Everyone looks to the side
as we walk up a few steps to the white bed
where two black baby girls lie on their backs
pushing with bare feet as they wheel around
one head. Their head's shared. They laugh up
at us, at the trailer, at the universe as babies do,
playing their game of going round the head.
They have pink bows in their braided hair,
wear starched white dresses. I stare so long,
standing there at the side of their two faces,
so close I could touch a shining cheek, that
Grandma has to nudge me. *There are people*
outside, waiting to see, she whispers. We leave.

Searchlights

Searchlights swing from the night horizon,
sudden and silent as heat lightning,
but not so bright, even the light hushed as it combs
the sky for enemy planes.

Somewhere, enemies get brushed with pale light
till the sky's clean as teeth.
Somewhere, searchlights are findlights. Meanwhile,
they make you feel guilty.

What if a searchlight came inside your window,
found you spying on the grownups,
listening to their conversation like metal ears of radar
lifted to overhear enemy agents?

What if you were one of them and had to be doused
with light till you went out like fire?
What if you were *behind the Iron Curtain* that fell in deep
dark folds like your black velvet skirt?

Sometimes you wish you were.
Backstage in the school auditorium is dusty, bare
except for chairs and costumes from plays. Being there
is like being nowhere, or anywhere.

Iron Curtain people throw themselves
out of windows, Ike says, because they have no purpose.
Having no purpose is the worst thing in the universe.
Is God backstage? The air feels emptier.

The Iron Curtain doesn't have a split
down the middle. It never opens
on a Christmas tableau or girl scouts getting badges,
things with so much purpose it hurts.

Adlai, 1956

Every other house on Oweno Road
has posters of Ike. We have you,
on our front door, Adlai. Huge.

Everybody knows Ike's a nice guy.
Everybody likes Ike. Even I do.
You don't look like you'd be nice.

You have small lips but a big mouth.
You laugh too much and not enough.
Adlai's a dumb name. Dwight is too,

but at least he gets called Ike. Why
can't you shorten to Ad or Lai? I
guess Lai wouldn't work. Besides,

you're not the nickname type.
I get sick of not having a nice
poster of nice Ike, sometimes.

It's not nice to come outside
and see you with your high
forehead and big, dark eyes.

I dream of you for years, when
you're at the UN and long after,
Adlai. I never dream of Ike.

The Living Room

For Thérèse and Wayne

I used to spy on you guys
twisting towards each other
on the loveseat where no one sat,
in the room where no one went.

When you danced sitting down,
when you danced with your mouths,
breaths warming that kept-cold room,
it melted around you, all that glass,

the figurines on little tables broke
soundlessly into a kind of rain
falling like light on the wood.
All sharp edges were tucked in.

I flowered down the aisle for you,
loving my own own bloom. Afterwards,
people flowed through the closed-off room
like it was open, always had been.

You drove away, the we of me,
in the car with its soap and tin cans.
I was left in my slippery blue dress,
your flower girl, in the living room.

Now the invitation comes to your fiftieth,
with the old picture against the fireplace,
bride like a white flame, smiling groom,
still living in the room. The living room.

Bobby and Pius, 1968

After he crossed the country by train,
the late Bobby Kennedy lay in state
in St. Patrick's cathedral, where the late Pius XII
stood in wax looking much as he had in life,

unlike Bobby who was strangely pale,
whose forehead was strangely uncreased,
whose lips were strangely sealed and thin,
whose hands were strangely icy and still,

at least not gloved and clasped but then again,
maybe they'd done that to him, steepled his palms,
wound a rosary in them? I doubted it,
not that I could see through the crowds of people,

stood backwards on an escalator across the street
to get a glimpse of the coffin in the dim space.
I couldn't see Pius at all but I knew he was there.
I wondered what Bobby had made of him.

I knew what Pius would make of the firebrand
who loved justice and Marilyn Monroe, although
at least he fathered a whole tribe of churchgoers,
who loved his brother's widow, though we didn't know.

We knew more about Pius and his hatred of Jews
than we did about Bobby and Marilyn or Jackie.
These things were hidden from the long weave of people
waiting to get into the cathedral,

but they were not deceived in him as we were in Pius,
turning yellow by the door in his ivory papal dress.
His passion was as far from sickly piety as Pius was from us,
that day when we paid our last respects, and lack thereof.

The Aunt

For Adele B.

Special buses swish us through the Bronx to
D.C. for The March. I'm here because of you,
entrusted to your care. You wear a shirtwaist
because they asked us not to look too radical.

You bring extra food, too, good stuff, to share.
Crowds cheer us on from sidewalks, a pulse beats
in my throat. The bus swings out of New York,
we sing *We shall overcome* and I, at least, am.

We march. We shake hands, talk to people, eat.
Then you order me to walk away, this is when
trouble might start. I hate you to King's cadence,
I have a dream in the background as we retreat.

- you are this contradiction, precise as a snapshot.
And so am I. Dissidence, obedience. In step, out
again. Teeth grit and grin. Life will never be easy, why
should it? But not even inside the skin, eh? Not even in.

Blue Hairbrush

Aileen Wuornos killed six men.
She was executed by the state of
Florida on October 9, 2000.

It's you at fourteen my mind rewinds to,
already absent from your neighbourhood,
but too present. It's dusk. Car doors slam. Food
smells carry on the still air-before-snow,
making you slaver as you duck and swoop
behind the houses. These people are good,
hard-working folk, they earn the aging Fords
garage doors shimmy away. They lie low
behind blue TV screens, they've earned their rest,
while you make your bed in a rustbucket
out in the woods, watching the big flakes star
the glass. Kids like you give good folks a test -
- their well-fed dogs bark as you pass. *Shut it,*
they mutter, but they all know who you are –

They mutter, but they all know who you are –
But hold that shot before it slips away
into the next – what if a neighbour came
down in her nightgown, moving fast like you,
listening for someone, forming an excuse
- she heard something – it's true – but in her face,
reflected in a darkened window pane,
she sees what she heard – it's her fleeing youth,
shotgun bride or not, by a hair's breath – why
not leave something, a kind of honest sop
to luck or grace that put her on this side
of the glass? Her hands shake, opening soup,
the edge of the tin can is too much like
the cervix, serrated by birth and God –

Your cervix, serrated by birth and God,
weeps clots, she knows as she leaves bags
with food, kotex – only white trash use rags.
But God's not on your side, and she did not
get up. The neighbours left you to your lot.
Later, you take a life after he gags
you, douches you with acid – as he sags
in the back seat, something gives up the ghost,
besides him – a faint shadow, growing blurred,
a Mason Dixon of the mind, made up
like longitude and latitude to tell you where
you are when you're at sea; only a word.
Something snaps, we say. Goes out of whack.
I can't help going back to that old car -

your road leads back to that old, leaky car,
becoming what you trust. Just cars and trucks
between you and the snow. Just men to fuck
between you and no food. I think that's our
road movie over. Who's the hitchhiker,
you or us? Would those damned metal struts
unpleating in the rewind, change your luck?
Who knows? You talk on camera from Death Row,
wearing the orange jumpsuit that's not yet
our state's emblem, tell your watching mother
- your blue eyes know she's there - a filthy whore,
then whip a small blue plastic hairbrush through
your hair. Standing at murder's door, you drawl
I have to freshen up into our stares.

Trees

For Adele

A few leaves blaze as we head down the thruway
towards Mahwah, New Jersey. Mostly they're green,
but there's an atmosphere of going, going - not quite
gone. Springsteen sings about the Mahwah Ford plant
closing down – I was there when Ford came in,

when Mahwah zoning for one acre was deemed
unconstitutional. Ford workers couldn't live
where they worked. Our father who art not
in heaven or anywhere else as far as we know,
explained it all to me, as I Ishmael it back to you

in the grey blur-stream of the thruway and the sky
through the windshield – we chew over the ironies,
passing over his thirty years' commute to maids on
downtown subways, migrant workers of the world,
on a righteous roll when we roll into Oweno Road,

where you never lived. One-oh-two is hidden behind
trees grown up past the roof, let alone the windows.
The door's obscured. The whole road's blocked off by
maples and oaks demonstrating against easy nostalgia.
Every house is Sleeping Beauty's palace, lost in trees.

I thought coming back made you feel like Alice after
a slug of *Drink me* grew her up. I feel like Gretel.
Where are the breadcrumbs of memory? Trees rampage
in the little island of green in the centre of town.
In three weeks it'll be a maple bloodbath. You laugh

the big fat chuckle you haven't exercised off.
I see we're on the way to Upper Saddle River,
zoned for two acres, the media res you came into.
Now I want trees. The big white house on the hill is

For Sale: it feels like a play, an afternoon soap:
What will the two sisters do, hunched in the car
on the West Road, snickering a little at the corny
detail of the sign on the lawn? Will they go in?

Knock at the door, pretend to be strangers,
find out, punch line, punch line, that they are?
Will they climb trees, break into the playhouse,
once the scene of sex, drugs, rock'n roll? (Not in my time,

Big Sister whispers). They fall silent. They sit,
not waiting for her to stroll down for the mail,
trowel in hand, with that sun-ironed look
that came before facelifts, from birds and dirt,

the calm before it breaks – not watching from inside
as he ducks under the pines, tired but glad to be home,
before he gets drunk. They sit and see nothing at all

behind the trees, not a shadow or a flicker
in the oak, maple and spruce, till it's time
to drive away, picking up speed, turning up Bruce.

Seeing Jesus in a Cheese Sandwich (Hollywood)

*After a piece that appeared
in the* Guardian, *Maundy
Thursday, 2005, about
unusual places where people
had seen the faces of Jesus or
Mary.*

Don't look at me I said, when He looked back
from a piece of bread, with Greta Garbo eyes
- *this ain't my kinda thing, I'm not your type.*
I took Him from the kitchenette to the deck,
hoping He'd evaporate. Carbs aren't on my diet,

you could say he saved me from myself. I ate cheese,
plain. It's ok on Atkins and South Beach, weighed.
I could play Mary Magdalene with long blonde hair
to my feet, massaging his – whore with a heart of gold -
but you get type-cast, What happens when I'm old?

- Thirty-five if you're lucky, thirty for most.
I'm twenty-nine. The next day He was still there,
eyeing me cheesily or goldenly, depending on your
point of view. Jesus, what was I supposed to do?
I put Him in the freezer, then thought: *ebay.*

Go on, say it, I'm Judas – Judy, actually.
Sold JC for a week in a spa, lipo, eyelid lift,
boob job, miracle cream greasing the palms
palmists refuse to read. I'm hungry all the time.
The Tarot showed the Hanged Man, made me scream.

Seeing the Face of Jesus in a Frying Pan (Texas)

Lived in the panhandle all my life,
panhandled some, in hard times,
down state. Don't shit in my own doorway,

or hang there waitin for a guy too tired
to take someone to dinner, get her high.
Later I come home, make pancakes with gravy.

Bit of a lady Peter Pan, well, not exactly lady,
not lately, anyway. Never could settle down.
Never could see what folks saw in it, even before

I got to know the men, how they gave up on
their wives in every way except leanin on them,
kinda like bein a wall. I stayed a window, I guess,

- more dangerous. Glass ain't stable,
that's a fact, kind of fascinating if you ask me,
looks fixed but it's fire and sand runnin away

like mercury between the frames. That's me.
Jesus paid me a visit one day, in the grease
left in the frying pan. That skillet held his face.

I didn't know what to do. Missed frying stuff.
He seemed to want some peace and quiet.
Always did like low-lifes, when you think of it.

Mary on the Glass Side of a Bank (Florida)

I'm a teller, tell it like it is. Try to.
You only get out what y'all put in.
Stopped a robber once with that sayin.
Wasn't expectin it. Most people are dumb?

Kinda tickled me, seein her up there
smack in the window of the bank.
That was rich. It made me grin all day
in my one-sided cage. Jesus, he drove them

money-grubbers out with a whip.
That's one way. But they always win.
She took another tack, his mother,
came to them, stained their expensive glass.

Seeing the Face of Jesus on an Oyster Shell (Switzerland)

A good bar runs like a watch
made of jewels that do what
nothing else can do for time,
diamond vodka, ruby port, gold scotch –

I like to greet the regulars,
help out in the kitchen,
make my presence felt.
Our bar snacks are seafood, pure protein

on the half-shell, fresh as
virgin flesh. It's a man's place.
One man I didn't expect
showed up like a bad drunk, had to be bounced

quietly, into my pants pocket
till I got home and had a chance
to examine him. I'd know that face
in hell, so close and faraway. I had it dipped

in gold on the Goldfinger principle
that anything alive would suffocate.
It's in my safe, a curiosity I picked up
somewhere in my travels, so my heirs will say.

Sounds like I've got it covered
but I listen at night, thinking
how *he* rolled back the stone –
not that I think he did, but you never know.

Besides, that face rises in front of me
all the time, white and pocked like
it was when I clocked it. Like beer foam,
only chipped and brittle. A good bar runs like a watch.

33

The Virgin Mary on a Leaf (Colorado)

Used to look hard at the world,
it was so big and unusual.
Got told off my whole life.

Folks get upset when you stare,
my mother used to say. *Don't.*
Lately I took to lookin down.

There she was, starin up at me.
Just hangin off the end
of a branch by a bare thread.

I stayed fer an hour, playin.
Havin a starin contest like two kids.
She's shakin and flutterin like anything.

Struck me she was plain laughin
to beat the band, not something
you'd anticipate. More like a carny gal

than *Our Lady*. Kinda hard, carved,
tatted up on the arms. Or the Fat Lady,
lardy, laughin in your face.

Old sugar maple stood there a century
before she started up, lips stained glass red
breakin' up at the whole fandango.

Nossir, I did not pick her. Press her
in a Bible, or the dictionary? What fer?
Next day, the tree was bare.

Laughed her own head off, I guess.
Might come back next year, like the carnival.
She was a good-time gal, a real one-woman fair.

Jesus in a Hubble Space Telescope Photo

Groupies to the stars, roadies hunched
over our instruments, that's astronomers.
Funny thing, I can't see Jesus in the printout
my colleagues made such a fuss about.

I see stars flash like the eyes of the senile,
pure feeling detached from any cause
they can locate. I see comets when they pass
like runaways who call collect from highways,

but I can't see Jesus in the picture,
and I guess he can't see me either, female,
riding that telescope like a witch. You see,
Jesus and me – we're not enemies, but we don't mix.

Seeing Mary on the Stump of a Freshly Cut Branch (California)

I chopped her off for Christmas.
Wasn't fussed about a tree,
what with the chemo.

Thought I'd have me
a nice clean branch, sniff it,
get that pine high,

but when I lopped her off,
it sounded like a hunka breast
droppin in a bucket.

Then I saw her lookin up,
this woman on the stump. They say
a hazel traps a witch,

but this was blue spruce,
not anything that sprang at
you like birch,

just held her face up
like a cameo, white and hurt,
calm. It drew me in,

I sat down in the dirt till
it got dark, then brung her back.
It makes a difference

that she stuck her face there
on an amputated limb,
just like my tit.

Don't bring it back. Never said that.
Just makes a difference.
That's it.

Jesus on the Church Door
(Massachusetts)

I'd been cleaning those doors for thirty years,
cleaning the floors till I could see
my face in them. I had my doubts, sure,

but I kept them down. Then came the day
I saw His face on the door we'd just had stained.
It was Him all right, pine-knots for eyes.

I started to cry, then I got my hat
and I walked away down the aisle,
turned my back on that pine-eyed god,

that was that. I had my sign. I never thought
He'd be so lacking in imagination
as to show up there, on a church door – fine.

The Virgin Mary in an Ordinary Window
(New Jersey)

She looks a little drowned up there,
adrift on the glass like a cloud –
I'd just had the windows done,
she's between new aluminium frames,
on a sheet of new glass.

I made a little noise at first – you know,
told people, had Father Ryan round.
He seemed uncomfortable, kept mentioning
Windex! –as if. Then I realised she was
a reflection in search of a rest,

a place to watch the world go by
and not be recognized. Lots of us get to
mooning in windows as we grow older,
looking at the crowds and clouds.
She's shy, tired, an aging child bride.

The Blue

It's gone the next day. Erased.
The sky's got its usual windows
of ice blue, shivery
but familiar. Last night,
a blue snuck up over the sea,
laced with silver, new to me.
I wasn't ready.
It wasn't cobalt or baby,
both scary enough, if you stop
to think. You don't. But this,
this was in my face. From the train.
Monday evening. Grey-breathed,
but awake. It, that is. Through glass.
Why did it blue like memory,
something you can't escape
or escape to? Will it return?
What will I do? Chase it? Run?
If it doesn't, I'll wait.

Tunnels

Hoods we put on nervously
like those about to be executed
but not like that. They never touch us
but we feel them, clammy stone weeping
through glass as we sit on the train,
taking us back as they thrust us forward,
always back. Always forward. There's no
sideways for us sidewinders looking for alibis,
it's either/or. You come in, you go out.
In between you wait while the river pours,
weaving the little track like Moses crossing
the Red Sea. Carving the mountainside
like the Pied Piper's chain of children.
Tunnels on dry land, free-standing,
come upon us like muggers, light
goes, phone signals, the world folds
into a stone corridor with no rooms.
This is not a place to be; to go through.
Over and over. Celebrated by street
singers collecting Charon forfeit as we
travel. Sweetening the journey, saddening
the way. They echo, tunnels, the acoustic
draws songs, sighs, screams. They go both
ways, to and from. We know there's light,
glaring, drowning us, at the end of one.

One Afternoon Sitting on the Sofa

All afternoon, I sat. I sat the afternoon.
The afternoon sat with me till it went away.
By then the afternoon was past, and I was up
about the night. By then it was about the night.
The lamps came on before it, like they do.

But afternoon held no lamplight. Clouds –
clouds did the three-dimensional thing,
some hiding behind others, drifting past
oblivious. A game like hide-and-seek,
the ones in front looking for the others,

not seeing them. I saw the whole scheme.
And then I saw myself peeled off myself
like a layer of cloud sliced, transparent,
like a blind fool – that was nothing new,
but I was a cloud too, moving or hiding,

a cloud that would pass, after rain
or before, some afternoon like this, as
someone else sat watching cloud-games,
feeling herself peel into layers of drift
with the same confusion as the clouds,

turning from Pegasus into a little pig,
inhabiting herself like a palace and a ruin,
but all of it cloudy, impossible to sift.
I sat all afternoon watching the clouds.
I knew how it would be. That I would, too.

Rhododendron

A rhododendron is a rhododendron is a rhododendron,
laced into a pink cloister of religious lingerie
the shade of a hundred flamingos taking off together
in a flood of wings. You're rooted in flight,
flaunt pink clusters like many-breasted goddesses,
each one a clump of nipples stuck together: the more,
the rhododendroner. I wore yours before I had my own,
lay on the dirt floor in your mauve cave, blossoming.

You lined suburban driveways then, made boundaries
that somehow overflowed like waterfalls,
staying in place as they spooled. You never pressed or chased,
remained respectful but real, didn't plead
for wobbly faith from me, or love, like God –
they said if He forgot me for a second I'd cease,
but it was He who flowered when I remembered,
wilted when I forgot, all-powerful but oddly weak,

his angels thin, anaemic things like white balloons
you had to keep on blowing up. You blew up your own
sticky flamingos, threw them on the ground when they went
brown. I practiced smoking with your rolled-up leaves,
committed the supreme sin, doing absolutely nothing
in your den of iniquity under those same lush skirts
breasting the Welsh hills, nippling the lemon air with sugar-tits.
I'm stealing time, doing what I did then. Rhododendroning.

Panic Stations

I guess popes don't spend much time in stations
hanging around waiting for trains, or in those
other stations of the mind that pass through
other lifetimes under sawed-off tunnels
twilit with half-regret – hence the papal bullshit
that Limbo doesn't exist. It's a moveable famine,
true, but you don't go anywhere without
passing through. Like being stuck between doors
in an airlock, marooned between buildings in
the airspace where nothing grows, all shadow,
no light. Stations bring it into cold relief, between-ness,
a condition somehow disgraceful, somehow degenerate
even, like something in a cocoon before it flies out,
breaking down, like something caught between sexualities,
on a margin where anything is possible, where the gender gap
means what it says, where there's no safe shore to land on
and the old dream of androgyny turns inside out
into this concrete floor at Lime St. or Victoria,
where Miss Prism's about to park a pram,
abandoning a child, a manuscript, a handbag –
behind the joke line, the vertigo, the urge to let go
as we clutch the handles that we hold – it could be Moscow,
this glass shell with its cold floor, waiting for
Anna Karenina to go under the wheels. Or Vienna,
where Sigmund Freud stands on the platform,
hating trains, hating his hatred of trains, thinking about
going *off the rails,* and other puns. Our little names,
our bits of paper with the date stamped firmly,
time stretching if you're early, contracting if you're late,
rails flashing and blurring like mercury -
the waver in the thermometer, not the little wing-heeled god
who doesn't visit stations – the hunt for drugs,
enough caffeine, chocolate, magazines to make you forget
you've forgotten something. Once I sat in magazine heaven

sipping cappuccino froth while the Virgin train burred,
when a siren bleeped us off again, into another pocket
of limbo behind the barrier where we stood orphaned
from our seats, our heat, watching police and firemen
flap in what was clearly a drill of some sort. *In case of
terrorist attack,* we decided, calmly; it was that time.
We chatted, complained, trooped back on
when bleeped, back to windows, stale magazines
we didn't fancy as we sat looking out
at the sides of rock that lined the way like city gates,
the landscapes we came into, left at the same second.

A Corner of The Artist's Room, Paris, by Gwen John

I think I married that room.
Its window wore white lace,
imprinted with the shadow
of a store at the end of the street

where I bought my favourite dress.
I would never find a better place.
Flowers in a glass of water
on the table were like faces

in a spectrum of solitude,
red, yellow, purple under
the eyes. I liked them
and the light they held,

that fell on the flat table.
I never tired of these miracles,
though the armchair's wicker
triangles complained a little

when I sat in love's favourite
shape, reflected in the eave
over my head. Inescapable.
My blue jacket, my parasol,

said I came and went alone.
It may be I painted silence.
It may be I painted with silence.
It may be silence painted with me.

Tracey Emin's Bed

Marcel floats by on his island of opium and mothballs,
choking on lime tea, lying on crumbs that stick him
like briars as he tries to follow his trick with the Madeleine.
As we do our two shipwrecks that pass in the night bit,
he raises an eye-brow, dark brown, twin to mine, in salute.

Downstream, Elizabeth chaise longues towards me, sipping
her own brand of laudanum and torturing the maid.
She sighs like I used to, before I died. I was a bitch too, once
upon a time. She's lace all over, makes me itch – one scratch
chases her, afraid she'll catch something. I hawk and spit.

Florence shakes her head, mimes wiping her chin,
half-sat weaving bandages of mist, fingers spidery as a pianist's,
on a stiff horsehair sofa she's made into a hawk's nest.
Better a basket case than a lady, she rasps as she drifts past.
I thought I was alone. I am, in an archipelago of mattress-folk.

Channelling Frida Kahlo

Come in, Frida Kahlo. I'm in a Provincetown boutique.
You're staring down at me from everywhere,
eyebrows in flight like Georgia O'Keefe's crows,
you know? You flirted with her. You flirt with me,
your heavy gaze says 'Come hither', imperiously,
like a goddess. Did you *find God in yourself?*
Did you *love her fiercely?** Your dresses cost.
Your skirts would rent a condo for a week.
You wore them to sweep over your hurt leg.
Your shawls – I can't afford to be you, Frida,
even buy a little matchbox shrine, a *retablo*
with your face inside. You hated Gringoland.
Your dress hangs on a clothesline
between a privy and a gold cup,
in your painting. You knew our two signs,
hygiene and success, our two idols. Will you show up
here on the beach behind Commercial Street,
collecting shells and stones in a basket?
Will you sit in the sand and smoke?
Will you float in on your raft of a bed,
stand posed like Huck Finn between posters,
laugh with the skeleton on top?
You never stood on your bed or jumped on it,
not after sixteen, flat on your back
as your first canvas entered the room like Gabriel,
demanding paint. Blank angels are best, yes?
Maybe you'll dash across the sand as a deer, your face
under her antlers, Sebastianed with arrows.
Maybe you'll be your own Pièta,
Madonna in corset with nails?
(She's bought a few of your pain-things) -
Will your hair be hacked off, thick,
a mass of black-green seaweed?
Will you come in bald and steaming,
sleek in a man's suit, swill from a bottle,

wipe your mouth with your hand,
rant about the second accident, the man?
You had a long convalescence with paintings,
lovers, trips, never recovered. Will we play
with dolls and monkeys, suck from each other,
sit cuddled against the wind, smiling and kind,
not go in till we've had enough, whatever that is?

*find God in yourself..... love her fiercely - from *For Coloured
Girls who have Considered Suicide when the Rainbow is Enuf* by
Noetzake Shange

Barbara Hepworth's Studio

I wanted stones, not bread,
a kitchen without rot. With dust,
instead. I wanted clouds and iron,
not ironing or white sheets on a bed,

a silence like the one that spread
in childhood when cakes rose
in the oven. That baked quiet.
I wanted it to hold, like wooden dolls

that fold into a wooden womb.
I wanted quickening to go on,
that wing-brush inside not
frozen but implied. I wanted fire, cold.

I wanted love split open
with blunt instruments like
nutcrackers and locked back up.
I wanted everything exploded and intact.

Georgia O'Keefe and Bones

Bones were an instrument.
You saw that right away, in
the white pelvis lying on sand,
a Jew's harp you could play.
Music came first, as it must.

Before shape, sound. Before
touch. Then pattern, on a quilt.
Then it fell into place. But the ache
of not being able to sing remained,
until you saw the bones lying bleached,

wind and light pouring through them,
whole skies of music waiting to be
composed by bones. Music comes through
what's old, not newly dead but long gone,
washed clean of death, sea-changed to

rich, strange light-trombones, trumpets
of afterlife. Some sanding down was left
to do, some washing, some housekeeping.
Then the waving of the baton at canvas,
waking the bone-flutes to their dance.

Charlotte Salomon's Anti-suicide Note

*Charlotte Salomon's mother killed
herself by jumping out of a window
in 1926, when Charlotte was eight.
Her own sister had drowned herself,
and four other members of her
family. Charlotte took on this
legacy in her autobiographical
work, Life or Theatre? and
overcame it. The Nazis murdered
her, pregnant with her first child,
in Auschwitz in 1943.*

I shrank the world to get a better look.
I was only a goldfish in a bowl.
I was only an actor in a role.
I made my debut in a picture book.
Look what I did, in the short time I took.
I shrank the glass, I heard the tale it told.
The window was a mirror, bare and cold.
It led me to the edge. My fingers shook.
Here is the stage my only mother chose
to stand on, glance a second at the stars,
and exit without leaving me a note.
I had to write my own. They were too large,
windows and mothers framed in them. I don't
- listen – become a victim, though it's hard.

Listen, I'm not a victim, though it's hard
to see through Nazi boots and Auschwitz fumes.
Try, please. I'm writing this last note to you.
I made a leap instead of jumping, dared
to paint the window and the woman pared
from living by her fingernails - see how
I poise her there in frothy white, one, two,
three floating female sails, three scars
bleached but insistent till the moment comes
when the pane shivers down between my hands
and glass turns into canvas I can stain.
My shroud turns blue to match the blue fathoms
I fish with pen and brush, needing no sands
but time's – and then the brutes take me away.

No time, because the brutes take me away,
ok, but get the point, please, of my nib,
paintbrush and life – don't let tears lie with glib
free-flow about my destiny. Don't let those apes
take what I did and was away with me.
I break the glass between me and my life.
I take a leap that keeps me from the brink.
- You either leap, or jump. That choice, I make.
A pale Ophelia drowning in the sky
pulls me towards her, but I row back
to land, a blue streak on the moving sea.
I leave a note refusing suicide.
Read it. My body joins the mounting stack,
my unborn child gone with me. Now weep.

The Bones

For Dolly

They dug the bones up after seven years
and oiled them, at least before
the Communists came and chased
your family from Rumania.
When you told me, I thought of dogs.

Now I see the point of digging up bones.
I'd do it if I could, tip into cold,
plain dirt the hard way, keep going
till I hit the shipwreck of a box,

the sunken lock, and find it picked.
I'd start in with my rag, wipe off
secret white sticks that hid inside
like dyamite, waiting for this.

Artificial Snow

For Wayne

Artificial snow, you tell me, is air and water,
add something about a fan. I stop listening,
convinced I won't understand, shade my eyes
to look into yours. I've just hugged you,
uncle light as a butterfly. You won't ski,
bones friable with cancer, but you load
the car, tell me about artificial snow
made out of water and air, somehow
whipped up with a fan. Then you hit the road.

The House

For Thérèse and Wayne

I lay on the floor in front of your front door,
inhaling cold air like your house was on fire,
the year it was all over with Dennis Hogan.

I liked your snow peas with mushrooms. I hurt
my father's feelings out back by your barbecue.
My mother sat in that chair. They're quiet now,

like fish in an aquarium inside our world
but separate, as if air turns to water when
you die and slowly you grow fins and scales.

They glide by, flashy but faraway, not asking
for attention. Once in awhile, one of them will
turn mermaid or sea-centaur, attempt the furniture,

half-sat, half-sliding back into the brine around
their half-smiles, washed-out eyes trying to focus.
They perch like hospital visitors, desperate to go.

Truthteller

For Gay

It wasn't the emperor with no clothes, not in our neck
of the woods. I always envied that kid. One shout
from the crowd and it's done. One hand over the mouth,

ok, maybe one clout, a few digs in the ribs, a shhhh or two,
no big deal. A *Wait till I get you home,* then the yell.
A few seconds in hell and you're a legend forever, a truthteller.

Something, widowhood or cancer, makes you answer,
take me through the winding passage up the long, cold steps
to where she sits and spins, the little witch who comes down

through the generations of women – or they come to her,
after long decades. You wait for me to see that waking
comes from the spindle's pinch, the pricked finger, not the kiss.

The Swim

For Amélie

When we swim your thick
milk chocolate pond
the long way round,
stroking out in front of
the grey house to
the half-moon of beach
on the other side, far enough
for you to feel across
from your life too,

we sit like seals and sun,
but unlike them,
expose our fears more
than our skin, these years -
our kids, we're fearful for
and of. Our men, ok,
fearful for. And of.
Our dead. Afraid they'll fade
or won't. In spring,

the baby ducks go under one
by one, you tell me,
snapped up by
turtles in the pond,
under the milk chocolate swirl.
How brave you are, as we
swim back, staying in range,
trying to decide between
a cup of tea and glass of wine.

The Prodigal

For Bill

You got the fatted calf, in case
you didn't notice. I flew across
the ocean, but you lit their faces.

It's bloody, the battle for status.
You were born male, got it gratis.
I fought tooth and nail, behaved,

became a good girl. You failed at
that game and I knew you'd won.
I used to cry in my room when

they screamed at you, hit out
at what would not lie down
and die the death of yes, wept

new tears when it seemed you'd
go the way of no instead. Now
you smile crookedly and I swear,

no one on this earth knows me
better than you. Or worse. It's
probably true, for what it's worth.

That Morning

Train cancelled, I head down
towards the prom for a walk,

stop at the little boating pond.
No tilting rudders, this Monday

before Christmas. But I'm struck
by the way one half is smooth,

one choppy, wind-cleavered
as usual – it takes me a second

to discern the fine hairline
that defines the pane of ice

sheered over the end closest
to the sea, the colder of the two,

it must be. The division is neat.
I go to the sea wall, where

frozen lips tell you *Be well,*
Be happy, spell out for me, too,

I love you. It's too late. I'm sorry.
I've been lying, or telling half-truths.

The Eucalypti

After you died, Father, someone sent a basket
of eucalyptus I inhaled like smelling salts, I guess,
like smoking stale menthol cigarettes stolen from
you, Mother, long ago. When you followed him,

I forgot the subtle smell of leaves called umbels,
but tumbled into the same well of grief. I bought
the two small trees much later, not knowing
they'd zoom up eucalypsing everything else

till they bent double in the wind, much suppler
than you two. No brittleness under their youth.
The strange thing is, I can't tell which is which.
Maybe you threw off those roles you played

like something out of Genesis, became late
bloomers in androgyny, hermaphrodites
after your time, posthumous trannies at least,
in your blue jumpsuits, laughing at each other

as you undid your zippers, silver and shimmering
outside the kitchen, two crazy kids doing the limbo
peeking in the dining room window, gleaming
and tossing like horses but more articulate,

as if you've kept the endless appetite for talk
you gave me - thanks, kids, I got the hot pants, too –
but also the hot lips, burning to talk, talk, talk,
through labyrinthine nights, that eucalyptic gift.

Wild Swans in New Brighton

We're walking on the prom and the word takes me
absurdly, the word prom and the swish of the sea
like net skirts, the taciturn surf frilling and flattening
brings back the tacky high of a white stiletto night,
billows of whispering chiffon, nests of arms –

undressing an inch or two of flesh at the neckline
- a dirty wavelet rolls back - was decadent, lush,
a kiss might hit a hot spot on its hit-and-miss hunt -
it spills, listlessly. There's no energy in this sea.
You were well sophisticated at fifteen, European –

two swans point like dogs, necks ruler-straight, bank
towards a see-through leftover slice of moon,
stretched full-tilt on potholed clouds, duck-feet point
like ballerinas', every muscle matched – they curve,
plash down on the marine lake with one swerve,

without a word. *Of course, they're birds*, you don't
reply to what I haven't said. Fluffed upright,
their squat feet keep the rhythm, paddling underneath.
I want one locked flight towards the same moon,
even a waning one. I want to dance on this prom night.

Electra's Therapy

Bloodshot face and eyes speak of the bottle,
- she thinks she's the Sibyl, with her *Closure*
and her *Moving On,* her ox-eyed daisies
in their Oxfam vase. *I never bring flowers inside,*

I tell her. *They only die.* She waits a beat,
red veins snaking over her cheeks like Medusa's
hairdo, then says as if it's a revelation,
They die anyway. Everything dies. I nod, add:

If we let it. She sighs. Her hand shakes a little
on the table between us. She hides it in her lap.
Don't be fooled by Prometheus,
I chide, *livers don't grow back overnight.*

I'm more of a Sisyphus type, she replies,
don't you think? We share uncertain smiles.
Silence blesses us. She looks tired.
The rapist, I remind her, *that's your title.*

Poor cow, she wants me to *adjust.* She smiles,
adjusts her spectacles. *Who do **you** want to be?*
Niobe, turned to stone for one father, instead
of fourteen children? Endless grief is egotism.

Your father lives in memory. Look for him there.
Mnemosyne, mother of the Nine, will mother you.
Take control – right now you're a character
in someone else's play. I clap my hands.

Great speech, Demosthenes. Now stick the pebbles
in your butt-cheeks. Do you see Medea, too? Oedipus?
Oh high end therapist to tragic heroes, heroines?
There is no other kind, she sounds tired, eyes the clock,

Time's up. Becalmed, I somehow make the door,
feel like I'm crawling on all fours; but she smiles,
bleats *Till next week, then; fare well.*
Outside, my sails deflate. I trudge parks, graveyards,

bent under my failure to mount the high altar
like my sister in her white linen shift, lift my throat
to the knife; or bide my time in exile,
like my brother. I want the queen's death, but what if

her murder brings endings to Euripides, Sophocles,
but not me? The white slice of my hymen,
splashed with blood like Iphegenia's white dress
might make a sacrifice – but what of the aftermath?

A matricide must fly the Furies always. The shift
from daughter to wife trades slaveries. She's ruined me
for sex and homicide, the bitch. I'll write my own obituary
if it kills me. It will. She'll piss herself, the Bacchanalian bitch.

The Rainbow

Like Judy Garland cornered by a fan
gushing against the flushing in the ladies' :
I love 'Somewhere over the Rainbow' so much,
Miss Garland - freezing her in the glass
as she snaps, *Lady, I've got rainbows up my ass.*

- I thought rainbows were for ladies -
sugar pinks, baby blues, soft-centred pastels,
restrained, restraining. Their Biblical pedigree,
a prophecy of terror to come, fire this time,
didn't help - the flip side of sugar is vinegar.

Then there was the cute pot of gold
at the end – I wasn't sold. One afternoon,
I happened on a rainbow on my way home.
It hung there, fixing me with third-glass burgundy,
yellow and green monk-brewed chartreuse,

cobalt of old lost certainties
and jockey silks, toreador's suits of lights,
a swash of diva hemline in the sky, making me
ashamed I'd ever failed to celebrate bad taste
belting out the blues like Judy, bruised, sublime.

Edgar's End

My father's end was mute.
No lines for him to lose,
bad actor that he was. Two
at the time, I watched him
blow away like smoke.

We never called him back.
Smoke's deaf, though
in sleep we couldn't help
but scream and choke
with grief, wrapped up in him -

Reprieve: *There was a long tumultuous*
shouting like the voice
of a thousand waters – you see?
and the deep and dank tarn at my
feet closed sullenly and silently over
the fragments of the House of Usher.

My mother, on the other hand,
could fly. Imagine the reproach
to *him*. Her end was red.
We danced around the bed,
trying to wake her. Where else get:

And the life of the ebony clock
went out with that of the last
of the gay. And the flames
of the tripods expired.
And Darkness and Decay
and the Red Death held
illimitable dominion over all - ?

My young wife bled out,
and the rest. Men drifted.
Women haemorrhaged.
My brother Henry floated
out to sea, returned and drowned.

Villains, I shrieked, dissemble no more!
I admit the deed! – tear up the planks, here
here! Here is the beating of his hideous heart !

Again and again, I confess to crimes
I commit in dreams. My pen repents.
A friend would put a gun to my head,
blow my brains out, I tell the doctor.
He drifts away down ivory corridors.

A voice in a white dress reads verses
from a black book I know, but do not
think I wrote. Is it my sister Rosalie?
Endings are my forte, I assure her,

but I falter. There has been no story,
only dread. No blame to my undead,
only to him who cannot plot his own
parting from what they call *himself*,

the master of suspense suspended,
more solid as the hours pass,
colder than any gas - is this my
last sentence? *Slowly, he froze?*

The Commute

I think you liked some of it, despite
the toll it took, as I go on knowing you

thirty years after your last commute.
Your life continues to unfold in me

uselessly, in love's extravagant way,
lavish when all is lost. I guess at you,

follow in your long silver tracks
most days, both ways. Routine

but intimate time, burrowing in
the seat, cosying to the window,

like sitting at a fire that smells of dill
and brine, watching the pickled world,

the shrivelled sea with its laugh lines,
the stream dangling its sitting ducks,

a drift of heron batting wings, not at
us, like giant eyeslashes, or huddled

on a fencepost in a sodden bundle,
a statue of Monday round the back

of B&Q, Tesco's, Birkenhead wetlands
I'd like to think you know through me,

but don't. Only your quiet liking of things
commutes to me, becoming more than love.